In Celebration of
Mihai Eminescu

FOREST
BOOKS
London & Boston

In Celebration
of

Mihai

Translated by
Brenda Walker with
Horia Florian Popescu

Eminescu

PUBLISHED BY
FOREST BOOKS

20 Forest View, Chingford, London E4 7AY, U.K.
P.O. Box 438, Wayland, MA 01788, U.S.A.

First published 1989
Second edition 1990
Third edition 1994

Typeset in Great Britain by Cover to Cover, Cambridge
Printed in Great Britain by BPC Wheatons Ltd, Exeter

Translations © Brenda Walker and Horia Florian Popescu
Illustrations and cover painting © Sabin Bălaşa

British Library Cataloguing in Publication Data

Eminescu, Mihai, 1850–1889
In celebration of Mihai Eminescu
I. Title   II. Walker, Brenda 1934—
III. Popescu, Horia Florian 1935—
859'.12

ISBN 1–85610–038–3 (cloth)

Library of Congress Catalogue Card No. 89–084143

Cover painting is taken from the mural
Nuntă Cosmică by Sabin Bălaşa

For the Romanian poet Ion Stoica,
Director of the Central University Library in Bucharest
who contributed to the birth of this book
with encouragement and support

Mihai Eminescu

Contents

(Brackets indicate posthumous publication)

Preface

by
Zoe
Dumitrescu-Buşulenga

Cultural history supports the theory that the Romantic genius has always struggled against time. Rising above the contemporary world, his sincerity, lofty thoughts and aspirations, inevitably bring him into conflict with society's conventions and prejudices, with philistinism and non-values, with misunderstanding and envy. Therefore posterity cannot help but view the Romantic artist as a hero whose fight and fall acquire tragic significance.

The dream of Eminescu's life is a direct result of this never-ending clash between the artist and his world. It began in his early years and continued until his death. As a young man he had an enquiring mind and a bold imagination; a proud figure who did not conform to the ethical or spiritual norms of those around him. The first clash came within the family, especially with his father, who, failing to understand his personality, attempted to direct him towards mediocre goals. From the age of fourteen he exerted his independence in many ways. An unusual love of truth and a horror of deceit, even conventional deceit, developed at an early age and perhaps formed the nuclei for the creation of Eminescu's attitude towards compromise: the first and necessary corollary of the noble ethical ideal which he lived.

Despite successive disillusionments, he believed in the capacity of people to achieve good, and to correct the evils that controlled society. This affirmation of an unswerving dominion of evil is present from his earliest creative activities, for in his personal life he was invariably humiliated and hurt by many mediocrities. In searching for good he found only evil. When he attempted to communicate at a certain level, people neither wanted to communicate nor knew how to do so. His thirst for absolute knowledge was confronted by the mediocre ambition of pseudo-intellectuals, and his desire for a better world was confronted by narrow-mindedness and malice. Such hostility and indifference engraved the impression of the supremacy of evil even deeper on the poet's heart. His intellectual training at the University of Vienna between 1869 and 1874, where post-revolutionary pessimism ruled unbridled, gave him a predilection for Schopenhauer's philosophy of disillusionment, and the theorising of renunciation, detachment and indifference. There is a fundamental contradiction between this philosophy of disillusionment (present in particular in the works of his maturity), and his uninterrupted and dramatic search for truth and beauty.

However, Eminescu was not inactive, indifferent or a recluse like Schopenhauer. His pessimism did not touch all the facets of his being, for his life, which he both loved and hated, was in full flow. He also hated imperfection, ugliness, meanness, lack of patriotism and stupidity, and in particular, petty politics with all its defects. In the poem 'Gloss' and in 'The Satires', although he preached indifference, he still had a great affection for the peasants, their values and their folklore.

One of the most important factors in Eminescu's life and personality was this link with the people of his birthplace. On his frequent travels he would make notes, record words, and old tales. The lyrical ballad 'Calin (Pages from a story)' and the philosophical poem 'The Evening Star' were inspired by such folklore. Even when abroad and gazing back towards his homeland, while adapting the oral literature which he had gathered for the expansion of Romanian consciousness and culture, he kept in mind the people he struggled to know during the period when he was a school inspector, a journalist, and a writer . . .

In respect of his political activity, he was never on the pay-roll of any political party, ready to accept a compromise. Throughout his life, his honour and moral integrity led him, at any risk or suffering to himself, to continue to serve his ethical ideal. Eminescu joined the Conservatives with one aim in mind, to serve the interests of the people intelligently, with perfect honesty and a skilful pen. He was drawn to the Conservatives through his terrible hatred of the liberals whom he saw as bitter enemies of the peasantry and of the old patriarchal order (as he preserved it in his imagination). While a journalist for the Conservative newspaper *Timpul* in 1877, these principal concerns often led him into conflict with the management.

With his artistic achievement he towers like a giant, but his artistry was born from a typically Romantic attitude: in youth, to overthrow and then reconstruct the world, in maturity, to control it through philosophical knowledge, through absolute knowledge.

Like every Romantic, in his desire to recreate the world on foundations other than those of a philistine and conventional thought or fantasy, Eminescu conceived beings unequalled in beauty and purity, who could regain their lost happiness seemingly outside of time and place. He created a profoundly original vision of the world which reunites him with the Romantic creators and yet singles him out amongst them. Giving cosmic dimensions to the laws of the objective world he built his own universe from folklore and ancient myths, fragments of which can be found in all his works. From cosmogony to apocalypse, the poets followed the most beautiful, and the grandest hypostases of life in all its elements. The sky and endless expanses of water, seen as fundamental sources of life, were those explored most consistently. The moon also fascinated Eminescu, not only for its strange nocturnal glow, but also as a planet unexplored by the human mind and thus offering opportunities for demiurgic control. Eminescu constructed new worlds upon it and with the richness of his imagination created many more suns and moons for the universe. Similarly driven by the thirst for beauty and happiness, he imagined paradisical landscapes in which people could rediscover their harmony, amid luxurious vegetation, surrounded by purifying water. Hence the richness of a generous, caressing nature in all its erotic lyricism. He then explored interstellar space with an equally boundless imagination, measuring distances in light-years ('From that Star'). He was immersed with Hyperion in galaxies and reached the borders of the active centre of the universe, symbolised by the throne of the Almighty. He discerned, in the light of the myth of the original creation, the first creation of eternal beings (according to gnostic or neo-platonic sources) as well as the second creation, that of ephemerally sad beings. He saw life springing from non-life in luminous swarms, and followed it stage by stage to the final development of the human form.

Love poetry occupies a large proportion of Eminescu's work. He attempted the complete realisation of his being in love as a corollary of his quest for the absolute. This supreme function of love emerges from the diverse aspects in which love accompanies the Eminescu hero, but in particular when the hero is an artist and creator (the Fourth and Fifth Satires). Failing to complete the great plan he had for the world and for society, and failing even more hopelessly on a personal and artistic level, driven by impulse and ideas in advance of the age in which he lived, he took refuge in various philosophies. Embittered towards the age, like all Romantics, he wanted to defeat it by endowing his heroes with magical attributes.

On the other hand he wanted to deny time, showing that the

dimension of the past and future are only illusory and that the whole of existence is a continuous present. In moulding his ideas he turned to Plato, Kant, the philosophy of the German Romantics Fichte and Schelling, then Schopenhauer, and Buddhist as well as neo-Platonist philosophy.

Reaching the dregs of disappointment, and the conviction that it was impossible to change anything in his own life or in other people's because of the evil which seemed to govern the world, he renounced it, consoling himself with such philosophical thought as is present in 'Gloss' and 'The Evening Star'.

Served by his knowledge of Romanian and foreign culture, and well read in Homer, Shakespeare and Goethe, as well as in Romanian folklore, Eminescu created a work which synthesises all these national and folk traditions. Only when you consider the deep roots of his background culture can the scale of Eminescu's linguistic contribution to Romanian literature be understood. The work of selecting and standardizing the language, uninterrupted throughout the poet's life, make him the greatest creator of language in our history and yet it cannot be separated from the enormous effort he made to discover the perfect form in literature. He cultivated the form so as to give it new values and new radiance. Thus a poem such as 'Tired Birds', whose words largely belong to the core vocabulary, is surrounded by that seductive, musical, expressive aura characteristic of all the poems written in

Eminescu's maturity, and suggesting the gradual settling of nature at nightfall and the sleep of elements which are almost personified.

Of course it is very difficult to understand a personality as complex as that of Eminescu, so full of contradictions and depth. The great breadth of his culture, his rare powers of movement at the height of human thought are still obstacles which we regard with respect and humility.

Unappreciated in his life-time, his destiny as a great universal poet is only just beginning a hundred years after his death, when his fellow Romanians draw closer thirsting for beauty and culture. We are attracted by his suffering as a man, his drama as a creative artist and his love for the Romanian people. Nothing expresses more accurately the link between this poet and his people, than the words which he himself wrote, in one of those moments of deep awareness:

> The God of genius drew me from the people, just as the sun draws
> up a golden cloud from the sea of bitterness.

These translations have given me particular pleasure, for they capture not only Eminescu's music but also his lyrical pathos. From the simple, genuine beauty of the fairy tale in verse, to the harsh shock of the satires, the original charm of romantic lyricism is preserved and cast in a contemporary English which enables it to pass directly to the soul and mind of our contemporaries.

The
Life of
Mihai
Eminescu

Mihai Eminescu was born in the village of Ipoteşti near the town of Botoşani on the 15th of January 1850. The family house was situated on a hillside with a panoramic view of other hills, valley, forest and lake. A church and monastery were nearby.

His great grandparents on the paternal side originated from Transylvanian peasants, but his mother came from a Moldavian family of country gentry.

Şerban (1841–1874)   Nicolae (1843–1884)   Iorgu (1844–1873)   Aglae (1852–1900)
Harieta (1854–1889)   Matei (1856–1929)

He was the seventh child of eleven children.

His father, Gheorghe Eminovici was a manager of a country estate. He was active in politics, able to speak other languages, had a liking for culture and books and was ambitious for his sons.

Eminescu probably attended the village school but was later educated privately by a German tutor. We are told that Eminescu and his brothers often played truant and that he disliked the harsh discipline of school life. He entered the third form of the National-Haptschule of Cernăuti at the age of eight and finished his studies there in 1860. The next stage of his education at the K.K. OberGimnasium lasted only two years and then he returned to Ipoteşti. He was sent back several times but eventually he evaded it by taking on work as a copyist at the Law Court of Botoşani. He never seemed successful at passing examinations.

The death of a teacher whom he loved and respected gave him the opportunity to enter the literary world with an occasional poem entitled 'The Death of Aron Pumnul'. He then made his debut in the Transylvanian journal *Familia* and it was here that the chief editor changed the young poet's name from Eminovici to Eminescu.

Eventually Mihai Eminescu left Bukovina and roamed through Transylvania and Walachia, working as a prompter and copyist for various theatrical companies, one of which was directed by Iorgu Caragiale. He also worked at the National Theatre in Bucharest.

Eventually his father sent him to study in Vienna. Here at the University he took a great interest in many things including Romance languages, medicine, political economy, physics, mathematics and philosophy.

It was here that various lasting friendships led him to contribute to the Romanian literary circles of his time and eventually he came into contact with the great literary critic Titu Maiorescu, a university professor and statesman (later Prime Minister in 1910–12). Maiorescu and the members of his literary circle believed they had now discovered the great poet of their epoch.

He returned to Romania, and Maiorescu persuaded him to continue his studies at the Humboldt University in Berlin with financial support from the Junimea, the literary circle. This he did for a time, studying history, Sanskrit and mythology, but he did not obtain a degree. However, he did prepare a novel (which was linked to the lectures he had heard on Egyptology), began to translate Kant, and undertook a study tour to research documents related to the history of Moldavia from ancient times.

Upon the sudden abandonment of his studies in 1874, he returned to Iaşi to become director of the University Central Library and a professor at the Academic Institute. This ended in a law suit over an alleged misappropriation of books. In 1875 he worked for one year as a school inspector, and then as editor of the *Iaşi Courier*, but lost both positions after coming into conflict with the administration. In 1877 he became editor and finally editor-in-chief of the newspaper *Timpul*.

During these productive years, his reputation grew as a fine writer, politician and journalist. His poetry became very popular and in 1883, Maiorescu prepared the first edition which appeared during the poet's absence from the country in December 1883. Unfortunately at this time Eminescu was not well enough to appreciate it, for he developed the inherited illness syphilis and his mental condition deteriorated.

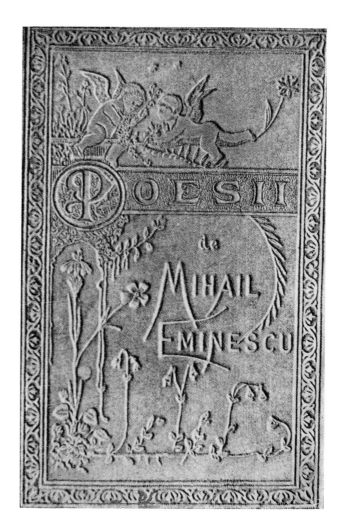

Eminescu's great love was Veronica Micle. Lovers before the death of her husband in 1879, Eminescu and Veronica enjoyed similar interests. She also wrote poetry and translated Edgar Alan Poe's novel *Morella* through a French intermediary. She was very beautiful and his love for her inspired a cycle of poems culminating in 'Calin'.

But while the Romanian culture was coming to self-understanding through Eminescu's poetry, the poet of the prayer from 'Ode' became estranged from his own nature, living a painful agony for six years, with lucid intervals when he was fully conscious of his illness and able to work a little. In April 1888, during one of these lucid moments, he accompanied Veronica Micle to Bucharest, resuming his journalistic activities and continuing his literary readings with his circle of friends. A year later, on the 15th June 1889, at the age of 39, Mihai Eminescu died. On the 4th August in the same year, Veronica Micle took an overdose and killed herself, saying that she could not live with the great void left in her life by the death of her great friend and poet Mihai Eminescu.

Translators' Introduction

by
Brenda Walker
&
Horia Florian Popescu

In Celebration of Mihai Eminescu

This selection includes only twenty-eight poems from the vast work of Mihai Eminescu, the great Romanian Romantic poet, who was one of the major voices in nineteenth-century European poetry. The number of poems is rather small, but we selected some of the masterpieces published during his lifetime ('The Evening Star', 'The Satires', 'Gloss', 'Ode', 'Calin', etc.) which can offer the English-speaking reader a fairly exact outline of the originality, depth and power of Eminescu's poetic genius. Our intention was to pay him our humble homage in this centennial year of his death. In this volume we have chosen poems which focus on the inner problems and anxieties of the genius, on the relations between genius and society, genius and love, genius and God.

For this translation we decided to use the three volumes of Eminescu's poetry edited by D. Murăraşu (Minerva Publishing House, Bucharest 1982). These texts are well established and justified within the research Murăraşu undertook. On the one hand, the editor has proved faithful to Maiorescu's edition (1883), and, on the other, he accepts the corrections made by other researchers when their arguments are convincing. This explains our omission of some stanzas in 'The Evening Star', as well as in the 'Fourth Satire' and 'Fifth Satire'. The omitted text did not seem to interfere with the aesthetic or contextual aspects of the poems.

Readers new to Eminescu's work may well be surprised by some of his extremely nationalistic verses ('Third Satire'), or by his attitude to women (especially in the 'Fourth Satire' and 'Fifth Satire'). His nationalism has a historical explanation. The Romanian provinces had for centuries been oppressed by several empires — Ottoman, Austrian and Russian. His burst of xenophobia was addressed to the descendents of such oppressors who, in his time, still held important social positions. Woman is worshipped like Venus or the Madonna in his splendid and tender love poems. However, he views his worship of chastity ironically when he dwells on other extremes such as the wanton, the fool or the whore.

Within this translation we have made great efforts to preserve both the outer and the inner music of Eminescu's vision. His poems are but parts of a magnificent symphony, a symphony of his feelings, thoughts and visions. With each poem we translated, we were made aware of its place in the context of the symphony through repeated images or vocabulary. Such repetition of rhymes, words and images can be seen in terms of music; parts of a grand whole which contribute to the overall vision. To complement this vision in the translation we used rhyming words like *he, she, his, her*, together with repetition of words like *night* and *light*. We also deliberately used *us, me* and *you* as suffixes to help capture the rising inflections of the orginal Romanian.

Translating poetry has always been a risky undertaking and it was not always possible to yield the fruit we were striving for. There are many debates on the interpretations of Eminescu's deliberate ambiguities and because such ambiguity was not possible in English, we had to choose. The exact translation of *Luceafărul* is 'Evening Star', but many translators have entitled the poem either 'Lucifer' or 'Hyperion'. Hyperion is the name God gives to the Evening Star towards the end of the poem, so we preferred not to use it until that point. The name Lucifer would have suggested the dual personality of man with regard to love: demon and angel, for there is a definite and careful balance of these two images within the text, and indeed throughout the 'symphony' as a whole. However, because the name Lucifer has so many different associations in English, it was felt that as the book was for an English speaking audience, it would be more appropriate to use Evening Star. Also the main theme of the poem is Eminescu's relation to the idea of genius. He describes it as follows:

> The allegorical meaning which I gave the poem is that genius knows no death, and his name escapes the night of oblivion. However, on the other hand, on earth he is not capable of making any one happy, or of even being happy himself. He is immortal but lacks good fortune.

An example of small ambiguities can be found in the fourth stanza of this poem. We chose to interpret *Luceafărul asteapta* as 'The Evening Star awaits her', rather than following the logical argument often presented, that she awaits her Evening Star, simply because it was better matched to the emphasis and music of the original.

As the Romanian language is so rich in sound patterns it was not always easy to find equivalences in the exact syllabic placing of the originals. We have deliberately avoided the temptation to invert syntax, use archaisms, or add unnecessary definite articles and other superfluous words (which would usually be omitted from a good English poem) in order to reproduce the exact notes of Eminescu's tunes. However, we hope that, overall, we have fulfilled the task we set ourselves, which was to present to the reader a faithful text rendered in a rich, musical equivalence which will provide not only enjoyment but a mirror where the beauty of Eminescu's work is, like the Evening Star, reflected timelessly into future centuries.

Acknowledgements

IN CELEBRATION OF
MIHAI EMINESCU

FOREST BOOKS wish to thank all those who have encouraged this publication and in particular:

The British Council for their encouragement and support

The School of Slavonic & East European Studies, University of London, for its support in the publication of this translation.

Centrala Editorială, Bucharest

Biblioteca Centrală Universitară, Bucharest

Dimitrie Vatamaniuc, director of research for the study of Eminescu at the Museum of Romanian Literature, Bucharest.

Sabin Bălaşa for permission to use the cover painting, and also for the black and white drawings which were created especially for this edition.

Zoe Dumitrescu-Buşulenga for her detailed introduction

Horia Florian Popescu for his untiring devotion to the task, and to those Romanians living in London who, for the sake of Eminescu, gave their precious time and valuable advice.

xl

BRENDA WALKER was born in 1934 on the 15th April in Liverpool. Her career has been divided between the arts and education, her university studies being at London and Keele. During the last few years she has devoted herself to poetry in translation working on Eastern European and Middle Eastern texts. Other Romanian titles have been co-translated with Andrea Deletant. Her own poetry is published by Headland Press.

HORIA FLORIAN POPESCU was born in 1935 on the 28th February in Bucharest. He was educated at the University of Bucharest and has a degree in English language and literature. At present he is a bibliographer at the Central University Library in Bucharest. His own publications in translation include works from such writers as Milton, Stern, Ginsberg and Mailer.

SABIN BALASA was born in 1932 on the 17th of June. His art education took place at the Nicolae Grigorescu Institute of Arts, the Italian Academy of Siena, and the Painting Academy at Perugia. Recognised as one of the most outstanding painters in Romania, he has also created films and animated cartoons. Winner of numerous awards, he has had one-man exhibitions in Russia, Egypt, Israel, Japan, France, Italy, Spain, Sweden, the Netherlands and the U.S.A.

Sara pe deal buciumul sună cu jale
Turmele l'urc', stele le scapără'n cale
Apele plâng clar izvorând în fântâne
Sub un salcâm dragă m'aștepți tu pe mine

Luna pe cer trece -așa sfântă și clară
Ochii tei mari caută'n frunza cea rară
Stelele nasc umezi pe bolta senină
Preptul
de dor, fruntea de gânduri ți-i plină

Part of the manuscript of 'Sara pe deal'.

The
Poems

Dusk On the Hill

Dusk on the hill, sounds of the long, slow alphorn,
Clambering flocks, sparks from the stars now landborne,
Streamlets weep, tears of crystal cascading,
There my love, under the willow you're waiting.

Saintly and pure, gliding, the moon's at its fullest,
While your large eyes gaze up to Autumn's harvest,
Dew stars are born, clear on the vault of heaven,
Peace on your brow, with longing your body is laden.

Clouds flow by, carving out light as it streams,
Straight to the moon houses stretch wooden beams,
Breezes creak the shaduf's arms on the wold,
Drifting smoke, murmuring pipes in the fold.

Tired men with scythes, carried high on the shoulder
Come from the field, calls from the toacă grow louder,
Ancient church bells well into evening's haze,
Love swiftly flares, my soul a white hot blaze.

Not long now and dumbness will strike the valley,
Not long now and then I'll have you near me,
All night long, hour upon hour I'll whisper
Under the willow, you will be mine forever.

Then you will sleep resting your head close to mine
And smiling we'll stay under night's counterpane
of vaulted willow – a night of golden splendour!
Who would not give life up for such a fine treasure?

Sky-blue Flower

"Are you deep again in the galaxy
In those clouds and the blue canopy?
Dear love, you must never forget me,
For your soul is life to me!

You build yourself images in vain
With lava rivers in the sun,
Plains of the Assyrian
Or the deepest, darkest ocean;

Time-worn pyramids, forcing
Massive peaks into the morning —
Don't go that far, searching
For happiness, my darling."

The young girl stopped chattering,
And stroked my hair smooth.
Ah! I knew it was the truth;
But just laughed, said nothing.

"Come where the wood's all green,
To where springs weep to the valley,
And the large rock hangs ready
To drop to the great ravine.

There close to the eye of the trees
Where the pool is calm and clear,
Under the still rushes there,
We'll sit on blackberry leaves.

And you'll say sweet words so wittily,
Your little mouth telling love-lies;
While I with a daisy shall surmise
How much you really love me.

And because the sun is burning
I shall be red as an apple,
And let golden hair topple
To stop those lips from talking.

And if you were to kiss my hair,
No one would ever discover
For it would always be hidden under
My hat, and who will care?

And when the moon is shining through
The branches of a summer night
You'll hold me in your arms, tight,
And I'll nestle close to you.

On a path under vaulted bowers,
When starting back home to the glen,
We'll kiss each other again and again
Just as sweetly as hidden flowers.

And when we reach the bounds of the gate,
We'll whisper together in the darkness,
No one will be there to worry about us,
Who cares such love is my fate!"

One more kiss — then gone . . . After
I stand, like stone in the moonlight,
Oh, how wild are those eyes, and bright,
And so blue, my sweetest flower!

And then sweet wonder, you left,
Love died after that hour —
My flower! My sky-blue flower!
And now the whole world's bereft!

The Lake

The blue lake of the forest
Patched now with yellow lilies,
Startled — rocks a small boat
In ever-growing circles.

And wandering along banks,
I half listen, half see
You rise up from the rushes
To lean gently against me;

Let's take the small boat,
And join the murmuring water,
I'll drop both the oars, my love,
And let loose the tiller.

Let's float, lost in the spell
Of the moon's hazy light —
The wind will whisper in the reeds,
Ripples sing for our delight!

But she never comes — Lonely
And in vain, I sigh and suffer
On the edge of that blue lake
With yellow lilies on the water.

Desire

Come now to the forest's spring
Running wrinkling over the stones,
To where lush and grassy furrows
Hide away in curving boughs.

Then you can run to my open arms,
Be held once more in my embrace,
I'll gently lift that veil of yours
To gaze again upon your face.

And then you can sit upon my knee,
We'll be all alone, alone there,
While the lime tree thrilled with rapture
Showers blossoms on your hair.

10

Your white brow with those golden curls
Will slowly draw near to be kissed,
Yielding as prey to my greedy mouth
Those sweet, red, cherry lips . . .

We'll dream only happy dreams
Echoed by wind's song in the trees,
The murmur of the lonely spring,
The caressing touch of the gentle breeze.

And drowsy with this harmony
Of a forest bowed deep as in prayer,
Lime-tree petals that hang above us
Will fall sifting higher and higher.

Calin

*(Pages from a
fairy tale)*

A Gazelle

Autumn — leaves go wandering,
In a corner — crickets singing,
Sadly, the wind taps the window,
Its hand trembling,
While you at the fireside
May well be sleeping . . .
Why do you start, when dreaming?
Someone's in the hall, creeping,
It's your lover coming
To clasp you round your waist
So he can hold a mirror playing
It on your lovely face, hoping
That you'll see yourself
Dreamily, smiling.

I

Over a hill the moon rises like a hearth full of embers,
Reddening the ancient forest, the tall lonely towers,
And waters from the river, which glitter, murmuring as they fall,

Descending to the valley is the sad toll of a bell;
On the edge of a high cliff, a keep's grey walls loom,
And up the scarp from rock to rock a young man dares the chasm;
On hands and knees along the craggs, from one ridge to another
Till finally at a rusted grille he breaks into the chamber
And creeps to a secluded bedroom past the silent stairway,
Enters — where the black wall froze into an archway
But the moon at the grating weaves her way through woven blossoms
To gently, very gently, shed the splendour of her beams;
There, where they reach — they seem to whiten floor and wall,
Where they don't — the shadows seem painted with coal,
And from floor to ceiling an enchanted spider has set
A thin web, spun as transparent as a net;
Trembling it seems to tear as the gauze gleams,
Sprinkled with a drizzling dust of precious stones.
The emperor's daughter sleeps behind this shimmering web,
Bathed in light as she lies there on the bed.
Her shape becomes full and white: with looks you could caress
Her body through the thinnest silks of such light lividness
For here and there an unfastened clasp will let the silk reveal
Her body in all its nakedness, white, pure and virginal.
The loose golden hair spreads out across the pillow,
A pulse beats at her temple like a violet shadow,
And then with a single touch a master's hand has painted

13

Arched eyebrows to complete her alabaster forehead.
Beneath her closed eyelids the warm blood throbs,
Languidly, over the side of the bed, an arm droops;
Ripened with warmth of youth are the berries of her breasts,
And her mouth opens a little from the heat of her breath,
She seems to talk in her sleep, smiling, with a sigh,
And on the bed and round her head scattered rosebuds lie.
And the young man comes nearer, and with his hands, tears down
That fragile web, scattering diamonds on her gown;
The gifts of her naked beauty so inflame his feelings
That the rooms of his mind almost flood with longings.
He looks down into her face and takes her in his arms,
Then as she sighs, with burning desire presses his lips to hers,
And takes the precious ring from off her little finger —
Then returns again to his world, this youthful stranger.

II

Next day she began to wonder at the torn bed-curtain,
And noticed in the mirror that her lips were blue and thin —
Then smiling and gazing wistfully, softly whispering she'd say:
"Shadowy youth with long dark hair, tonight steal me away."

III

Everyone has his own view when it comes to young girls —
But she resembles those who are deeply in love with themselves.
It was Narcissus, who, using the brook for a mirror,
Adored his own reflection as if his own lover.
And if someone were to come and take her by surprise,
When she looks in the mirror with those large, wild eyes,
Calling her own name by pursing her small mouth,
Fonder of herself than anyone else on this earth,
Then he'd confirm her illusion with the brightness of his glance,
This beautiful girl had found the spell of her own radiance.
Oh you, idol, thought's ecstasy! With large eyes, lovely hair,
What a wonderful idol you've chosen for your virgin desire!
What is she whispering secretly as she looks in astonishment
At her tender young body, from head to foot?
"Such a dream I had last night. A shadowy youth came to me
And I thought I might have killed him by clasping too tightly . . .
So when I gaze in mirrored walls that reflect all my charms,
And am alone in my room, I stretch out white arms,
And in my delicately woven garment of golden hair
The sight of my bare shoulder tempts me to kiss it there.
But then shyness draws me back, a blush comes to my face,
Why doesn't my shadowy lover come for me to hide in his embrace?

If my body is lithesome, and I admire my eyes and beauty,
It's because I know that this will also make him happy.
And I'm fond of myself because he's fond of me —
Now remember dear mouth! Betray me to nobody,
Not even to him at night when he nears the bed like a demon,
Cunning as a child, full of longing like a woman!"

IV

Every night he comes again to the bed of the fair princess.
But one night she was awakened by his charmed kiss;
And when he turned to the door to steal quietly away
She stopped him with her eyes, and then he heard her say:
"Oh stay, stay with me, sweet lover with long, black hair,
For your words are tender fire, luckless shadow of the air,
Don't look so lost and lonely, for in this world you'll find
There's a young soul waiting for you, loving and kind.
Oh, passing shadow — with such deep looks that seem to sigh,
So sweet are the eyes of your shadow — God forbid the evil eye!"
He seized her round her waist as he sat by her side, perhaps
She whispered words burnt by the fire from her lips:
"Now whisper to me," he said, "you with your pagan eyes,
Sweet meaningless words, full of meaningful sighs.
The golden dream of life is like lightning, an instant

But when I touch the roundness of your arm, I'm in that moment.
When you count my heart-beats by resting your head against me,
When I touch your smooth, white shoulders to kiss them passionately
And when our breathing becomes one and is part of my life
And when my heart swells with yearning, with such sweet grief;
When in ecstasy you press your burning face close to mine,
Binding my neck with your hair, so fair, so fine,
When you half close your eyes to bring my lips such pleasure,
That happiness I feel is just impossible to measure.
You!! . . . See I'm so tongue-tied, I can't even name you
Or say how much, oh, how much I really love you!"
They whispered, saying many things, not knowing where to start,
Stopping words with a kiss to quench the other's thirst;
Clasped in each other's arms, they kissed trembling,
Their tongues became silent, only eyes went on talking,
Until blushing from shyness she hid her face with her hands,
And her tearful eyes behind those thin golden strands.

V

That face once rosy as an apple, is now not quite so fair,
But grown pale as wax, thin enough to cut with a hair,
And you gather up to your eyes your long fair tresses
You, heart without hope, a soul tormented by memories.

CALIN

Standing day-long at the window, you only weep and sigh,
Until you glance through long wet lashes to let hope soar high
With a lark who flies swifter and swifter into the blue,
You wish she'd take a message to your lover for you.
But the bird flies away . . . your dark eyes, still weeping
Stay with your open lips that ache with trembling.
Don't waste those young eyes, stepchildren of the skies,
Don't forget that teardrops give the mystery to blue eyes.
Stars rarely fall from heaven, like the silver dew,
And tears sit well on the canopy of blue;
But if every star fell, the heavens would be sad and empty,
You'd no longer be able to gaze upon so much beauty —
A night of stars and moonlight, of rivers reflecting light
Is a long way from a coffin's dreary, desolate night;
And tears shed from time to time can quite become you,
But if you drain away their source, how could he see you?
A blush, lovely as a rose, flows right through them,
And also the bluish snow of your thin cheek comes from them —
Not only their blue night, but their sweet eternity
Could so easily be wasted by crying aimlessly . . .
Who would be so foolish to allow an emerald so priceless
To fade, burning all its glitter to dust for no real purpose?
Your beauty burns up in your eyes . . . Their sweet night is fading,
And you're unaware of the world's loss. Don't cry now, stop weeping!

20

Oh, Emperor, you with the knotted beard like uncombed wool,
You're quite devoid of reason and your head's an empty shell.
Are you happy to be alone, you foolish old ruler,
Sucking away at your pipe sighing for the loss of a daughter?
Counting as you walk the white planks of the tower,
Once you were very rich, and now you've grown poor!
You not only sent her away, far from her parents, but
Made her give birth to a royal child in some painted peasants' hut.
Now you send messengers far and wide hoping that you'll find her,
But she hides away in a secret place and nobody knows where.

VII

It's a grey autumn evening; the grey water of the lake
Has smoothed out its wrinkles and the reeds no longer shake;
And the woods gently sigh and a sudden gust of wind
Charges through the dry leaves scattering them on the ground.
Ever since the forest, that dear forest, piled its leaves,
Opening up its thickets to the moon's sleeves,

Great sadness has descended, just twigs the shy wind breaks,
And waves of gurgling drift from lonely rippling brooks.
Who's coming down from the forest so late in the day?
A young man who scans the valley as sharp as a bird of prey.
It's seven years since you left, shadowy lover with long dark hair
And you seem to have forgotten the proud maiden you thought so fair,
And on the deserted plain he sees a barefoot child walking
Trying to coax back to his flock one unruly gosling,
"Good-day to you, Lad!" "And to you, stranger,"
"What's your name, boy?" "Calin, like my father;
That's what my mother says, when I ask again and again,
— Your father was a shadowy youth and his name is Calin."
On hearing the boy, he knew at once that this was his own child
And the storm burst in his heart, beating loud and wild.
Then he entered the hut and saw on a bench in a broken dish
A dim light from the blackened wick of a burning rush;
Two flat cakes baked in the ash of the chimney's floor,
A slipper thrown across a beam, the other behind the door;
The old hand-mill lying useless in the corner by a shelf,
And on the floor, purring, a tom-cat washing himself;
Under the smoke-darkened icon of a blessed saint
A light, small as a poppy seed, burned constantly, but faint;
Also on the icon shelf were basil and dried horsemint
Which filled the gloomy place with a strong sweet scent;

On the clay-coated oven and on the peeled-off wall
That dear little child had painted piglets with some coal
Paw-like sticks and curly tails that showed good breeding,
Just how all pigs should look if they've had good upbringing!
An ox-bladder instead of glass covered the little pane
Where a gloomy yellowish streak of light filtered through the stain.
The young mother sleeps on boards with a rough sort of pillow,
And in the stuffy darkness, she turns her head to the window.
The young man sits beside her, and soothes her brow gently,
He touches her sighing, then caresses her sadly,
And bending close to her ear, whispers her name softly,
And she raises the long silken veil of lashes sleepily,
She gazes at him in fear . . . thinks it a dream. He can't be there!
Afraid to smile lest he vanish, she'd cry out but does not dare.
He lifts her from the bed and holds her closely,
He thought that he would die, his heart beat so violently.
She stares again and again, with eyes laughing and tearful,
Yet never utters a word, as if frightened by a miracle.
She twines his long hair round her thin white finger, then
Hides her blushing face as she nestles up against him,
He unties the kerchief to let her hair cascade down,
Then kisses her soft hair at the parting of the crown
And lifts up her chin to stare at eyes brimming with tears,
As they stop each others words with kisses full of desires.

Once you've passed copper forests, the horizon becomes whiter,
And you hear the wondrous voices of those proud woods of silver,
Then, near springs, the grass seems like snow there
And wet blue flowers shiver in incense-ladened air.
Perhaps souls are hidden in the bark of ancient trees
Whose voices are felt whispering high up in the leaves.
And through the impressive darkness of the silver woods
And on glow-glittering stones you can see shattered brooks;
Then gently sighing past flowers they ripple down busily,
As they descend the hill's steep slope, gurgling sweetly.
They throw their water-balls onto backwater pebbles,
Into nest-rings of water where the full moon settles.
Thousands of small blue butterflies, thousands of swarms of bees
Cover flowers full of honey with their glittering seas,
The humming celebrations of the forest insect choir
Help fragrance and coolness to fill the summer air.
Near the lake which throbs sleepily and gently pulses,
Look! There's a table laid with brightly lit torches,
From the four corners of earth they've gathered at her side,
Emperors and empresses, for the wedding of a bride;
Charming princes with golden hair, scaly dragons clad in armour,
Wise men, soothsayers, and Pepele, the travelling joker.

And the Emperor, the bride's father, leans back in his chair,
A crown is on his head and his beard is combed with care,
He sits erect, sceptre in hand, leaning on feathered pillows
While pages guard from flies and heat, with branches from the willows . . .
But look, at the edge of the forest, where no guests stand,
Calin the bridegroom comes, leading his bride by the hand,
There's a dry rustling of trailing leaves under the long white dress,
Her cheeks glow red as apples, eyes full of happiness,
And almost touching the ground, her long gold hair quivers
Falling about her arms and over her bare shoulders.
And so she approaches, gracefully, her noble bearing happy now,
She has blue flowers in her hair and a star upon her brow.
The bride's father has invited proud guests to join them soon,
The sun to sit as best man, and as maid of honour — the moon.
And they all take their places according to age and honours,
As the pipes set up a tune accompanied by the fiddlers.
But what's this noise? It sounds like bees swarming?
All look around amazed, to see what's happening,
When they suddenly see from the shrubs a great cobweb bridge,
Where bustling crowds of small creatures cross from edge to edge,
Look at the ants carrying large sacks of flour to make
A great baking for the day, as well as the bridal cake;
And the bees carry honey and a fine dust of gold,
For the beetle, master goldsmith, will make ear-rings, I'm told.

Now the new wedding procession comes — a cricket's the best man,
Before him, fleas with steel shoes jump as high as they can;
A big-bellied bumble bee clad in velvet for the feast
Intones through his nose a jangling song, just like a priest;
The cobweb bridge shakes with the locusts' nut-shell carriage,
In it, with twirled moustaches, a butterfly bridegroom goes to his marriage;
Butterflies of every kind, thousands follow him and his family,
And all are so light-hearted, very jocular and jaunty.
Then come mosquito fiddlers, small beetles and many more,
While the bride, a shy violet, waits behind the door.
Onto the Emperor's table jumps a cricket, with livery shining,
And rising on back legs bows so low his spurs start clanking,
He clears his throat, buttoning his elegant vest, then after a pause,
"If you'll allow us, Noblemen, our wedding will take place with yours."

CALIN

Over Tops of Trees

The moon steps over tops of trees,
Leaves beat gently against the firs,
And from branches of the alders
A melancholy alphorn grieves.

So far off, so far off,
Very slow and very faint,
It makes my body long for death
Easing my troubled heart.

But now, why are you silent
When my spell-bound heart is torn?
Will you ever play again, sweet horn,
To recapture that moment?

I Don't Believe in Jehovah

I don't believe in Jehovah,
Or in Buddha — or in Vishnu,
Or in life, or in death,
Or in extinction, as some do.

They are only empty dreams,
And it doesn't matter to me
Whether I live forever on this earth
Or vanish into eternity.

All such holy, pious secrets
— Mere words with a hollow ring —
You try to understand in vain,
For thoughts won't change a thing.

And because I don't believe
In anything — Oh, give me some peace!
I shall do just as I like,
And you just as you please.

Don't try to change me with classics,
Or with the old and pedantic,
I don't care about any of them,
I remain what I was: a romantic.

So Far Away From You

So far away from you and lonely by the fire,
I think about my luckless life while sitting here,
I seem to be eighty, and feel that I've lived
As long a time as winter, — that you're already dead.
Memories seep drop by drop into my soul,
Awakening within me what was once trivial;
The wind taps against the pane with its fingers,
The thread of tender moments is spun and lingers,
And there through the mist you again go past me
Tears in your large eyes, slender hands, icy,
With arms round my neck, you stay clinging
As if you'd something to tell me . . . then you're sobbing . . .
Such treasure of love and beauty I hold close to my heart,
United in kisses, sad lives kept apart . . .
From now on let the voice of memory always be silent,
So I'll never again remember that chance moment,
For after that moment you tore yourself away . . .
I shall be old and lonely, you dead for many a day!

Oh, Stay

"Oh stay here, stay with me,
For I love you so much!
I'm the one who hears your longings,
I'm the only one you trust;

In the eery haziness of twilight
You seem to take the disguise
Of some prince who fathoms water
With his deep, sad, dark eyes.

For against the sound of rough waves
And grass bowing low to the crags,
I've helped you hear in secret
The canter of passing stags.

I've watched you, a changeling,
Humming softly in a dream,
While stretching out a naked leg
To the sparkle of a stream.

And when you see the full moon
Across the cold blaze of a lake,
Your years seem only moments,
Sweet moments long years take."

Said the wood, in a hushed whisper,
As its arches swayed above me —
In answer I just whistled
Then rushed out merrily.

But today even if I did return
I'd only hear the emptiness.
Where are you now, childhood days,
Your wood, all you possess?

Years have trailed past . . .

Years have trailed past like clouds over a country,
And they'll never return, for they're gone forever,
And I no longer enjoy such light endeavour
As the magic of folk songs or the land of faery

Which as a child filled me with wonder,
Not quite understood yet meaning so much to me,
And now these shadows try to recapture me
In this hour of mystery, this twilight hour.

These trembling fingers touch the strings in vain
To find the right notes from the fading memory
Of youth, so that my soul can vibrate again.

Everything's disappeared from the horizon of that distant plain
And you can no longer hear the voice of past harmony.
Behind me time gathers . . . and I darken!

A Dacian's Prayer

When there was no death, nor immortality,
Nor any seeds of light for life's entity,
There was no today, or tomorrow, yesterday, or forever,
Because life springs from one and everything was together,
When the whole earth, the sky, the air, and sea
Were among those things which had yet to be —
There was only You! So I find myself asking:
Who is this god to whom we're all praying?

He was alone, the only god, there was no other
And for life's spark drew power from vastness of water.
He gave souls to other gods, and happiness to his creation,
Remaining for mankind the source of their salvation:
Lift up your hearts! Praise him in your belief,
He is the death of death, the resurrection of life.

And he gave me eyes so I could see the light,
And a heart that filled at every pitiable sight.
I heard his footsteps when the wind was whining,
And his loving words, in the voice of a song, —
But despite all these gifts I have one more request:
Allow me the gift of eternal rest!

Let him curse all those who now would pity me,
Let him bless those determined to oppress me,
Let him listen to any mouth that wants to insult me,
And put strength into the arm that's about to kill me,
And make first among men, he that when I'm dead
Would rob me of the stone they place at my head.

And let them chase me through life, let them harass me
Until I feel the tear ducts of my eyes empty,
And each man in this world to be my sworn enemy,
Until I no longer recognise my own body,
Until feelings turn to stone after so much agony,
Until I curse my mother, whom once I loved dearly —
For if cruel hate turned to the love that I deny,
Perhaps I'd forget suffering, and then could die.

Let me die a stranger, alone in banishment,
Let them throw my worthless corpse wherever they want.
Let the dogs rip out my heart, and to the man who incites them,
To him, Father, — give a golden diadem.
But the one who would stone my face to disfigure me,
On him, Lord, take pity. Let him live eternally.

And only then can I thank you, dear Father,
For allowing me the chance to live on this sphere.
But I'm not going to kneel and plead for gifts from you,
Just hatred and curses are what I really beg of you,
And to feel that in your breath my own breath will cease,
Then vanish in eternal emptiness, without trace!

Now it's
autumn . . .

Now it's autumn, leaves roam and scatter,
Again the wind flings heavy drops against the glazing;
And you're reading old letters, tattered and fading
And retrace a whole life-time in just one hour.

With sweet trifles you enjoy such time-wasting,
You'd hate to be disturbed by a tap on the shutter;
For when it's sleeting outside, it's so much better
To dream by the fireside, sleepily nodding.

So I stay in my chair, staring into the fire,
Dreaming of old tales and a fairy queen's sighs;
Around me the mist rises higher and higher;

Suddenly the rustling of silk makes me rise,
Steps so soft, barely touched by the old floor . . .
Then with slender, icy hands — you hide my eyes.

Time flows by . . .

Time flows by, and has passed like rivers
Since that hallowed moment we first saw each other,
Yet I'll never forget the love we had together,
You miracle, with large eyes and cold fingers.

Oh, come back! To bring words only you can inspire,
Watch over me so your gaze gently lingers,
Let me marvel at this moment that hungers
For those new words you wring from my lyre.

You're not even aware that when you're near
A great peace descends to quell my agony,
Just like the silence at the rising of a star;

If I could only see you like a child, smiling up at me,
All the suffering of my life would disappear,
My eyes rekindle, my soul grow within me.

Oh, Mother

Oh mother, sweet mother, from the rustling of the lime,
Let me hear you calling through the darkness of time;
From above the black stone of this sacred tomb
Autumn and wind cast willow leaves down,
I hear your voice echoed by the branches' gentle tapping . . .
Boughs will tap forever, forever you'll be sleeping.

When I am dead, my love, don't sit and cry for me;
But break a bough from the sweet lime tree,
And then above my head bury it with care,
Letting your eyes shed every tear-drop there;
One day upon my grave I'll sense a shadow growing,
That shade will grow forever, forever I'll be sleeping.

And if by chance it happens that both of us should die,
Within the rough stone they mustn't let us lie,
Let them dig our grave upon the bank of a river
And place us in the room of our coffin together;
And then as before, near my heart you'll be nestling . . .
The water will weep forever, forever we'll be sleeping.

From the Multitude of Masts

From the multitude of masts
Setting out with seagulls' cries,
How many will be torn apart as
Winds rise, waves rise?

Of those migratory birds
Filling land and sea with cries,
How many will be drowned as
Waves rise, winds rise?

If you throw away good fortune
Or ideals, likewise
You'll be followed everywhere, when
Winds rise, waves rise.

The subtlety of what you write
They'll never recognize,
Yet your song will sing in flight
As waves rise, winds rise.

The First Satire

When at night with heavy eyelids, I put out the candle's flame,
Only the old clock follows the winding path of time,
For when you draw the curtains, through the pane, there's the moon,
Showering her voluptuous light on everything in the room,
And from the night of recollection she stirs what might seem
An eternity of pain, we feel only as dream.

Oh moon, lady of the sea, you glide on the world's vault
And fade out many sorrows by giving life to thought;
Thousands of deserts, Virgin, glitter beneath your light,
And how many forests hide sparkling springs from sight!
And what myriads of waves are covered by your dominion,
When you float on the rolling solitude of every ocean.
So thrilled by your own magic you're eager to see palaces,
Just how many flowery shores there are, and great cities!
How many thousands of houses you enter gently through the glass,
How many foreheads full of thoughts, you stare at as you pass
You see a king that studs the globe planning for a century or more,
While the poor hardly think of what tomorrow has in store . . .
Though drawn for different ranks from Fate's lottery on earth,
We must all submit alike, to you and the angel of death;
All being slaves to the same string of passions,
Whether weaklings, powerful ones, geniuses or cretins!
One searches in a mirror for the locks of his youth,

Another searches the world and the eyes for truth,
Gathers husks in thousands from paper's faded leaves,
To notch up tallies of some short-living names;
Another will share out the world over shop counters,
Checking gold the sea carries in her black ships' lockers.
While there an old scholar, jacket sleeves worn out,
In an endless calculation will count and recount.
He buttons the old gown at his chest, shivering there
And plugs his neck in his collar, and cotton in his ear:
And scraggy, a nobody, hunched up, just a scholar,
He has the universal mystery within his little finger,
For behind that brow, future and past come into being,
A series of numbers, bringing eternity to understanding,
Like Atlas who in ancient times bore heaven on his shoulder,
He also bears eternity and the world, but on a number.

While the moon shines brightly over piles of tattered pages,
Instantly his thought carries him back down the ages,
In the beginning, when there was nothing, nor anything moving,
The earth was without form and void, void of willpower or the living,
When there was nothing to hide, though everything was hidden . . .
When the infinite rested, impenetrable and forbidden.
Was there a chasm? A gulf? A vast expanse of ocean?
No mind or eye could grasp or see the signs of any motion,

For there was only darkness like a sea without a glimmer,
With nothing to be seen, and not a being to see it either,
The shadow of the uncreated wasn't ready to disperse
And in harmony with herself the ruler was eternal peace! . . .
But suddenly something stirs . . . a dot — the first. Look, there! . . .
How a mother is born from chaos while he becomes the Father . . .
At this point of movement, far weaker than a bubble of froth
Will be the boundless sovereign of each world henceforth . . .
Since then the eternal darkness has divided into bands,
Since then the world has risen, with elements, sun, winds . . .
Since then till this very moment colonies of all lost earths
Come from grey valleys of chaos following unknown paths,
And springing from the infinite, brilliantly lit and swarming,
Are lured into life by their boundless longing.
And within this large world, we, children of the smaller
Pile anthills on our earth, one after another;
Microscopic people, kings, soldiers, scholars,
Each succeeding generation considering themselves marvels;
One-day flies on a micro-world we measure precisely,
And within all this boundlessness we whirl, totally
Forgetting that this earth is but a frozen frame of light,
That behind and before it, all we can see is night.
As the dust plays in the realm of a ray of sun,
Thousands of blue-violet grains vanish with it again,

So into the night of eternity forever deepening
We hold the moment, we have the sun, that's still lasting . . .
But when it goes all will go like a shadow in the darkness,
For the chimeric universe is but a dream of emptiness.

You'll find that no deep thinker ponders on today,
In a moment he shifts forwards in time thousands of years away,
The sun, which today is splendid, he sees as sad and red,
How it closes like a healing wound in clouds overhead,
How all the planets freeze and dash rioting in space
Broken loose from brakes of light, and the sun, in their chase,
And the world's icon screens sink blackened in that void
And like autumn leaves all the stars begin to fade;
And time stretches its corpse to be endless duration
For nothing happens now in this lifeless desolation,
All things fall silent into this night of nothingness,
And reconciled with itself, regains eternal stillness.

Beginning with the lowliest of creatures from serfdom
And climbing life's ladder to the heads of the kingdom,
We see them all tortured by the enigma of life,
But can't say for certain who will get most strife.
As their lives spring from One, there is the will to exist,
And he who can will certainly rise well above the rest,
While others more humble stay behind unknown,

And lose themselves secretly like unseen foam —
And what such people think or want — is nothing to blind fate
Who sweeps humanity wave after wave, just like the wind's flight.

Let all you writers praise him, let the people come to know him . . .
Yet what will the old scholar gain from all this mayhem?
Immortality some might say. It's true as you can see
That he clung to one idea in life, like ivy clings to a tree.
"If I die," he says to himself, "my name will be dispersed over
The centuries. From mouth to mouth, they'll carry it further.
Forever more and everywhere in some corner of a brain
My writings will find shelter under cover of my name!"
Poor wretch! Isn't it possible your memory's mistaken
About everything that you've seen, heard, or ever spoken?
Yes, it's possible! There are only fragmented images getting fainter,
A mere shadow of a thought, or a note on a scrap of paper,
And when you can't recall your own life off by heart,
Who is going to strain their wits to find out just a part?
Perhaps some pedant with greenish eyes, after an epoch
Will pour over wretched books, while he himself's a wreck
In order to appraise your mind and your great atticism
Blowing scornfully from his glasses, dust raised by your wisdom.
And you'll be gathered up in two lines, then sent remote
To the end of a stupid page in some idiotic footnote.

You can build a world or destroy it . . . but whatever you've said
A shovelful of earth will still be thrown upon the dead.
The hand that sought the sceptre of the world, and the thoughts
Which embraced all creation, find room within four boards,
They'll all follow to the cemetery in the funeral procession,
Splendid, like an irony, and with indifferent vision.
And raised above the others, some creature will say a few
Brief words about your work — appears to give his own view
Under the umbrella of your name. What more do you expect
For you see . . . posterity will appear to be even more 'correct',
And if they can't be your equal, will their praise come naturally?
Of course they'll applaud such a subtle biography,
In which they'll try to show that little of your work mattered,
That you were a man like them . . . And so everyone is flattered,
You no longer overshadow them. And nostrils so foolishly
Distended, dilate pompously in such a learned company
When it's you they're speaking of. You see they'd already agreed
That with ironic grimaces they would only praise your word,
And so fallen into wrong hands you'll have a certain flavour,
What's not understood they'll blame on your endeavour.
And what's more, they'll scrutinize and analyze your morals
To find blemishes, misdeeds and all the petty squabbles.
And each defect will bring you nearer . . . not the light
You brought to the world, but the sins and the guilt,

The weariness, the weakness, every evil which must
In the end link fatally with a handful of dust;
Every small petty squalor of a soul that's been tormented
Will attract them more, far more, than anything you created.

Between walls, and among trees that are losing all their blossom,
How the full moon spreads quiet splendour on her dominion!
And from a night filled with memories thousands of longings stir,
But because they seem a dream, their pain's no longer there.
For in our inner world she moves the door from the lintel
And arouses many shadows when we've blown out the candle.
Thousands of deserts, Virgin, glitter beneath your light,
And how many forests hide sparkling springs from sight,
And what vast numbers of waves are covered by your dominion
When you float on the rolling solitude of every ocean,
And all who are subjected to the powers of fate on earth,
All must submit alike, to you, and the angel of death.

The Second Satire

Why is my quill left lying idle in the ink, I hear you ask?
Why tempting rhymes don't lure me from yet another mundane task?
Why they sleep stuck and immobile between yellowed sheets of paper,
Lilting iambes, and trochees, all those dactyls which should caper?
If you only knew the problem of this life I struggle through,
You'd see I have good reason now to break my quill in two,
For why should one start, trying to make trouble
By recasting the wise, old language into a new model?
To display like goods for the theatre in a rhyming couplet
Those feelings that dream in your lyre, that delicate secret,
While you're frantically searching for that form you're after,
To have to write for that mob some syrupy words on water,
But, I hear you answer, it would be fine if my name
Were to rise through beautiful verses giving everlasting fame,
Attract attention to myself from the nation's men of substance,
Dedicate my verses to their ladies, for instance,
And bearing this in mind I can quell my soul's distaste.—
My dear, such a path has already been paced;
Our age already knows those strange bards who try
Through their various 'works' to climb up high,
Dedicating verses to the great and to the ladies,
So they're boasted in salons, and friends sing their praises;
On finding the paths of life so narrow and difficult,
They try to cross them under cover of some petticoat,

58

Dedicating books to ladies whose husbands they're hoping
Will soon become ministers and help them get an opening. —

Are you asking why I resist the temptation of glory's greatness?
Can you really call it glory, when you speak in such a wilderness?
Today when every mortal is a slave to his own passion,
The glory is just a fantasy that a thousand fools fashion
For they see an idol as great, though he's nothing but a pigmy,
A bubble of froth floating in a worthless century.
Shall I restring my harp to sing of love? Fetters
Shared as brothers between two or three lovers?
What? Humming on a sweet string, admit you joined the chorus,
And willingly sang in an opera conducted by Menelaus?
Nowadays, like the rest of the world, woman is often a school
Where you learn only grief, pretension and how to be made a fool;
And in such academies of the Goddess Venus' science
One finds them now enrolling even younger and younger clients,
You see them receiving beardless students in their classes,
Until the whole school is turned to dust and ashes.

What! You remember the academy where we'd sit and dream,
Those years when old teachers mended the garment of time,
Bending to gather corpses of moments from old and bulky volumes

59

And searching for wisdom in life's tattered costumes.
And through their gentle murmuring, a source of *horum-harum*
Discovering sleepily *nervum rerum gerendarum*;
And with reverence they managed to drive our minds to things
Swaying over a planet, or the old Egyptian kings.
I can see him now, that astronomer, with the eternal peace of darkness,
How easily, as from a box, he drew entire worlds from chaos,
Stretching black eternity before us, so we'd come to understand
That epochs are strung together just like beads on a band.
Then the vast world would turn like a windmill in our head,
So we 'felt the comedy move' as Galileo fearfully said.

Dizzy with planets, dead languages and dust from desk and cloth,
We mistook our poor teacher for a knight gnawed by a moth
And gazing on the ceiling at spiders' webs and flies,
We listened to King Rameses and dreamed of blue eyes,
And we wrote sweet verses in the margins of the paper
Addressed, for instance to a rosy, wild Clotilda.
And blending with the ages they floated, intangible,
Yet, there was a king, there a sun, and there a domestic animal.
This calm was enchanted by the busy scratch of quills,
We could see green waves of wheat and fields of flax on hills,
All vanished to infinity when desk rested heavy head;
The bell rang, and then we guessed Rameses must be dead.

In those days, the thought world was our reality,
While in contrast, the real one, seemed an impossibility.
Only now can we see the way so arid and hard,
A path rarely suited to an honest heart;
And in that vulgar world to dream is dangerous,
Illusions will find you, lost and ridiculous.

And so from now on, from this moment, please remember not to ask
Why tempting rhymes don't lure me from yet another mundane task,
Why lilting iambes, and trochees, all those dactyls which should caper
Still sleep stuck and immobile between yellowed sheets of paper . . .
You see I'm afraid that if I go on writing verses,
My dear contemporaries might start singing my praises.
Though their hatred I could handle with a light dismissive gesture,
Adulation, that's decisive, would offend beyond all measure.

The Third Satire

A Sultan, one of many, who ruled firmly over nomad tongues,
(Shepherds, who when seeking pastures, changed homestead and lands),
Pillowing his head on his right arm slept out in the open
But with his eyes closed on the outside, the one inside is woken,
He sees the crescent moon descend gliding across the horizon
To come very close to him transformed into a young virgin.
 As if touched by the feet of gentle spring the pathway blossoms,
Though her eyes brim with shadows from all her secret sorrows;
Stirred by so much beauty the forests are quivering,
Waters start to ripple — translucent faces trembling,
Powdery diamonds fall to earth as fine as drizzle,
 Floating through the air till all nature starts to sparkle
And through this wonderous spell rang the music of sighs
And the rainbows of night stretched up to arch the skies . . .
Sitting down beside him, she moved with delicate caresses
Letting dark hair fall loose in fine silken tresses;
"Come to me, my love. Let me bind my life to yours,
And relieve my sweet sorrow with your strength and sorrowing years . . ."
It's written by stars and time, there in the book of Life
That you shall be my Lord, and I — your wife.

As the Sultan stares, she darkens — slowly disappearing:
And from his loins he feels the shoot of a young sapling,
Grown in an instant as in a century, and keeps on growing,

With its branches over the earth and the sea still spreading,
And embraces all the horizon with its gigantic shade,
And within its shadow the whole universe starts to fade:
And in four parts of the world he sees ranges of mountains,
Atlas, the Caucases, Taurus, age-old Balkans;
Sees the Euphrates, the Tigris, the Nile, the old Danube —
The shade of that proud tree becomes King of the whole globe.
And so Asia and Europe, then Africa with its deserts
And the black ships in full sail rolling on the rivers,
The green waves of wheat rolling across the lands,
Seas upon seas bordering cities on the strands,
As on one vast carpet . . . they're all laid out together,
He sees country next to country, one race near another,
As they loom from milky darkness and unite their destiny
In a vast and great empire, under the shadow of that tree.

Even eagles soaring high cannot reach the top branches;
But a triumphant wind now begins to breathe through the ages
And lashes again, and again those resounding leaves,
Cries of "Allah! Allah!" can be heard from clouded skies,
And the uproar swells ominously like a turbulent ocean
And great shrieks of battle seem to collide in fierce commotion,
And scimitar-like leaves are blown towards a new Rome
Where they bow down in prayer before their holy, golden dome.

The Sultan shudders . . . awakes . . . and in the night-cooled air

Sees how the full-moon floats upon the field of Eski-Shehr.
And as he gazes longingly at the Sheik's house in shadow,
He catches sight of a young girl behind the grate of a window
Who smiles at him — as slender as the branch of a hazel;
She's Malcatun, the Sheik's daughter, young and beautiful,
And then the Sultan knew that his dream was from the prophet
That he'd ascended in this dream to the paradise of Mohammed,
And that from his worldly love an empire would be born,
Whose boundaries and years were known by heaven alone.
The dream takes shape, stretches out like a vulture
Year after year the empire grows larger and larger
And the green banner rises above many a conquered nation
Who by destiny must follow, race by race, Sultan by Sultan.
Country by country surrenders to the glory of the victor,
Until the tempestuous Bajazet reaches the Danube river.

On command, they're binding boat to boat till bank to bank is bound
And the whole army crosses this bridge while trumpets sound;
Janissaries, spahees, all Allah's adopted sons
Come to darken Rovine on the open ground of the plains,
Spreading row after row, they set up their tall tents . . .
The only sound is murmuring from the forest of oaks in the distance.

Look! A kerchief on a stick there's a messenger coming slowly,
Bajazet, looks hard at him, and then asks scornfully:
"What do you want?"

                "Us? Peace be upon you! And if he may come
Our Sovereign would like to meet the glorious Sultan."
On command, the way lies open, near the tent a man appears
Seemingly quite humble, plain in speech, bent with years.
"Are you Mircea?"

             "Yes, Emperor!"

                        "Do you come to kneel to me
Hoping to keep your crown, and avoid a thorn-wreath destiny?"
"What you will, mighty Emperor, whatever your intention
But while we are still at peace, I sincerely wish you welcome!
As to the question of submission, my Lord, please forgive me,
But do you intend to chide us now and lay waste our country,
Or perhaps you will reconsider and your Imperial steps retrace
Thus giving us some token of your majesty's grace . . .
Whether one or whether the other . . . in the end the fates decide,
Be it peace or war, we'll bear our lot with pride."

"What? Do you think that when the world is for the taking
I'd let a stump like you send the Osman empire tumbling?
Oh, you can't imagine, old one, how they did their best
To bar my way. All those proud flowers of the West,

66

Those in the shadow of the cross, emperors, and kings, intent
On joining to oppose this hurricane raised by the Crescent.
Clad in shining armour were the knights of Malta,
And there was the Pope with his triple crown, preaching from his altar.
Gathering lightning against a lightning that was even stronger
Who had conquered lands and seas in his tempestuous anger.
If Rome but winked an eye or beckoned them hither
The whole western world wanted to become a crusader.
For the victory of the cross set them flowing like rivers
Flushed out of forests or summoned from the deserts,
Disturbing even the deep peace, from the creation of worlds,
Darkening the horizon with tens of thousands of shields,
They advanced creating terror like a wood of swords and spears,
And the sea, with its sails, shuddered beset with fears,
At Nicopolis, do you remember how camps gathered to enrol
To stand firm against me like an undefeated wall . . ?
When I saw that multitude, thick as leaves, thick as flies,
I muttered darkly in my beard with such hatred in my eyes,
Then I swore a mighty oath to mow them mercilessly down
And to feed my steed on oats at that altar raised in Rome.
So you think a rough staff will protect you from my hurricane?
And do you think, driven by victory, I'd stumble over an old man?"
"An old man, that's so Emperor, but I am no commoner
This old man here is the sovereign of all Wallachia.

For your sake I hope you'll never feel our power
Or the seething foam of the Danube river.
Many have been here in the course of time starting with the one
Who was mentioned in chronicles, Darius, the Persian's son;
Many attempted at different times to cross this river,
They tried with great armies, they brought great terror;
Emperors whose ambitions could hold them home no longer
Came here to this country seeking our land and water —
And believe me, I don't intend to boast or frighten any one,
But they returned to land and water just as fast as they had come.
And you brag about marching, and destroying like thunderbolts,
Those armies clad in coats of mail, emperors, valiant knights!
You boast that the western world strove to silence your deafening thunder!
But what urged them to do battle? Please tell me, what were they after?
It was to tear from your iron brow that coveted laurel wreath,
Each knight determined to triumph in defence of his faith.
As for me, I defend our needs, our people and our poverty,
And the river, the trees, anything that moves in this country
Will remain a friend to me, but to you — a ruthless enemy,
And you'll not even be aware, yet soon will feel their enmity.
We've no huge armies, just love for a homeland, so don't forget,
This is a wall your fame will never breach, Bajazet!"
The old man had hardly left, when — what a roar, what tumult!
The forest seethed with sounds from weapons and trumpet,

At the skirt of the trees many long-haired heads started
Out from the dark shadows and thousands of helmets glinted.
On command, the horsemen charged, dashed to the field and spread
Spurring with wooden stirrups to give wild steeds their head.
Hooves hardly touching the surface of the blackened ground
Lances shining long in the sun, bows strung in the wind,
And like the patter of hail and clouds of bright copper
Arrows spring from everywhere making the sky much darker
Whizzing like a hurricane and the sharp snap of rain,
The field roars with clatter and shouts of sudden pain.
Vainly the Emperor shouts like a raging tiger
As the shadow of death grows wider and wider,
Vainly he raises the green banner waving it as he rides
His armies threatened by death, and surrounded on all sides,
Long lines of battle stagger thinned out as they yield;
The Turks fall in throngs scattered like chaff on the field.
Far off horses are felled, foot soldiers sink to knees
While waves of whistling arrows are speeding through the skies.
And striking face and back like an icy wind around them,
On the field they sense the whole sky shattering above them.
The Great Mircea himself leads the furious hurricane
Which rolls and goes on rolling trampling all who came,
Riders come roaring with a tempest of tall spears
Splitting apart the pagan troops in wider and wider paths.

The enemy's lines are routed, scattered totally

And the country's flags appear in an endless wave of victory,

Like an enraged sea or an overwhelming deluge of power.

The pagans like winnowed chaff are blown within the hour

Driven to the river's banks by a hail of steel's defiance,

While the glorious Romanian army stretches far into the distance.

While the army is settling, the sun is going down

On the country's high peaks, yearning to crown

Them with haloes of glory, long flashes of petrified light

Border the black mountains with the on-coming night,

Until one by one the stars appear from the depths of ages

And from the mist between the wooded slopes, the moon rises.

This lady of night and sea, sheds lasting peace and slumber,

Beside his tent, a son of the great victorious king ponders

As smiling, he rests a letter on his knees, remembering her loveliness.

The letter he'll send to his sweetheart's home, not far from Arges:

> I'm speaking my dear lady,
> From Rovine's dark valley,
> By letter, not by speech this day
> As you're still so far away.
> I ask you, with all my heart
> To send me that which you are part
> The forest with its clearing,

71

The valley with its spring,
Your smiling eyes beneath your brow,
And in return I'll keep my vow
To send you all that's fair to see,
Our banner with our army,
The forest and its leafy rooms,
The lofty helmet with its plumes,
Have no fear for I live heartily,
Thanks be to Christ, our Lord so Holy,
I kiss you, my Lady, sweetly.

The chroniclers and minstrels were worthy of such times:
Our century is full of imposters and Herod-like crimes . . .
Only in old manuscripts can real heroes be found;
How would the stories of today's patriots sound
With the music of the flute, the lyre or the cello?
Oh, you had best keep hidden from their sight, Apollo!
Oh, heroes! Once you were ignored overshadowed by the past,
Now you're in fashion and they pull you out at last
To drape you on fools, with quotes every blockhead knows
Dredging the Golden Age with cloying mud of their prose.
Stay in holy shadow, you noble founders
Of the nation, who gave us laws and were creators
Of customs, who with plough and sword set the land free
Stretching from the mountains, to the Danube, then the sea.

And present times — aren't they fine? Haven't I all I need from them!
Aren't I sure to come across someone who's a splendid gem!
Aren't we near the temple of gloss at Sybaris?
Don't the streets and coffee houses find us fresh glories,
Aren't there people fighting with sharp rhetorical weapons
In the loud approbation of street gangs and villains
Those who juggle the country's affairs, who walk on high wires,
Actors wearing famous masks in the Comedy of Liars?
Doesn't the liberal speak of motherland and honour
You'd think his private life was no less than crystal-pure?
And you'd never dream that he's a coffee house hero
Who plays with words noisily, scoffing as he does so.
Over there's the monster, without mind, without soul,
Eyes overhung by bushy hair, puffy lids, swollen jowl,
Dark looking, greedy, hunchbacked, a source of tricks,
He tells his venomous trifles to his fellow crooks;
Virtues spring from all their lips, but they only show
False coin, quintessence of squalor from top to toe,
And the monster with frog-bulged eyes stares keenly
On everyone that's around him, surveying his army . . .
And it's from these that my countrymen choose men to represent them!
Such people should be safe behind the walls of an asylum,
That levy taxes, make laws and speak with fake philosophy,
Wearing shirts with long sleeves and night caps set jauntily.

The Patriots! The virtuous, founders of establishments,
Just debauchery's froth, their gestures and arguments,
And as Saints in pews they sit with the piety of foxes
Frantically applauding grimaces, songs, obscene dances . . .
This spittle of poisoned froth, this mob, this scum,
Are now in power and rule our Romanian nation!
Those in neighbouring countries considered idiots or misshapen,
All that nature marked with the stain of something rotten,
All that's treacherous and greedy, all the Phanar, all the helots,
Were all disgorged into here to become our patriots;
So that snufflers, bubblers, simpletons, the goitrous,
And stammerers with crooked mouths are now our nation's masters,
So you're the descendants of Rome? You, the impotent, the wicked?
Human beings should be ashamed to think themselves related!
And this plague upon the world and all grotesque creatures
Have no conscience as they chew with their foolish features
The glory of our nation, discrediting it without shame,
They even dare to pronounce our motherland's name!

In Paris, in brothels of cynicism and stagnation
With its obscene orgies and its coarse lost women,
You gambled all your wealth, youth too at a cost . . .
Yet how could the west find gold when there was only dross?
And then you returned home with a jar of pomade for thinking,

A monocle for spying, and a walking cane for fighting,
With the brains of a young child you're all prematurely maimed
A waltz learned in a ballroom being the only knowledge you gained.
And in exchange for your wealth you have the slipper of a whore,
Oh, progeny of Rome —, how I admire you, more and more!
But now you look afraid of our sceptical old eyes,
You're astonished we are no longer taken in by your lies,
For we have seen these people, so great at talking,
Chasing only money, profit made without working,
And when their polished prose no longer deceives today,
It's others who are guilty, gentlemen. Well aren't they?
Now you've shown your true colours, tearing up this nation,
You've made our people suffer enough shame and condemnation,
Too long you've mocked our language, our forefathers and customs
But now at last we see you as you are — Villains!
Yes, profit without work, that's your constant passion;
Virtue? That's stupidity; Genius? What misfortune.

But at least let our ancestors sleep with the dust of chronicles;
From past glory they'll peer ironically at your monocles.
Why not come back, Vlad Tepeş, to gather them up again,
Herding them into two cages: villains and the insane,
You could drive them all in fury till they reach the dungeons' wall,
Then in prison or asylum — just set fire to them all.

The Fourth Satire

Lonely, the castle stands, and is mirrored by the lakes,
Its ancient shadow sleeps in the clear waters' depths;
Surrounded by firs it rises silently in the glade,
And over the rolling waves casts an ever-changing shade.
Through arched windows, beyond the panes, one can see only
The flutter of long, draped curtains, like frost twinkling brightly.
The moon trembles on the forest, kindles, grows, starts to rise,
Outlining all the tree-tops and hills against the skies,
And oaks appear like giants to safeguard her leisure,
Watching as closely as they would a hidden treasure.

Only the white swans, set sail from reedy darkness,
Reigning over the waters as guests of their stillness,
To shake their outstretched wings and pierce its mirrors,
Now in circles of tremors, now in a blaze of furrows.
The tall reeds rustle as the roaming waves pass by,
And from the flowering grasses, drowsy crickets sigh.
The summer air is scented and so sweet is the murmuring . . .

Only the knight below the balcony, stares up sighing
At a bower so cloaked in leaves, that through the balustrade
Red roses tangled with creeper, fall in a rich cascade.
Drunk with the evening and the breathing of the water;

His guitar spills out sweetly over the charm of nature:

"Oh, come to me once again, in your long silken gown,
Whose folds seemed laden with a fine silvery down,
I'd gaze for the rest of my life, admiring your wreath of moonshine,
While your white hand smoothes the wisps of your flaxen hairline.
Come! Play with me a little . . . with my fortune . . . and from there
Throw me from your breast the wilted water-meadow flower,
So it will touch and waken every string of my guitar.
Ah! The night is as white as if there'd been a snow-shower.
Or let me come to the scented shade of the secret room you're in,
There to be overcome by the smell of fine linen;
Cupid, the playful page, will hide the light's violet globe
With the palm of his hand, lithesome mistress of my soul!"

And the silk dryly rustled on the floor near earthen jars,
Among red roses of Shiraz and blue liane flowers;
Then she leans over the trellis, her smile, ethereal,
The young girl laughs, to her beloved she's an angel;
From the balcony she flings a rose and cups her hands firmly,
She seems to be chiding him, yet whispering warmly,
Then she disappears a moment . . . you can hear her descending . . .
Then quickly she comes out, arm in arm they're standing.

77

Hand in hand they walk. How well they look together,
She is beautiful, he is young . . . so suited to each other,
And from the shadowy banks the boat is steered past
With both its white sails hanging loosely from the mast,
And it advances eerily with slow strokes of oars,
Rocking all the enchantment and beauty on the shores . . .

The moon . . . the full moon comes, she rises also fair
And linking strand to strand creates a pathway of fire,
Where quickly, that girl of gold, the dream of eternal darkness,
Stretches out over small waves whose numbers become endless;
And while her sweet light grows clearer and clearer
The waves and the bank seem to rise ever higher,
The forest's growing larger, and appears to come much nearer
Together with the full moon's disc, sovereign of the water.
Lime trees with vast shadows, blossom-laden pulled to earth,
Gently shower wind-swept petals to the darkened water's path;
Over the girl's fair hair, the petals fly, rain, and then
She winds her little hands around his neck once again
And leaning back her head, "Don't talk, love, say no more . . .
For your words sound oh, so fiercely sweet to my ear!
With the pain of your soul my only real adornment,

This poor slave is raised to your thoughts' firmament.
Your voice's gentle fire gives sweet pain, yet thrills me
So it seems that at times we are part of some old story;
All those dreams, and your eyes express such sadness,
That my mind's consumed by their humid blackness . . .
Don't turn away, my darling . . . to rob me of your eyes' fire,
From the sweetness of their night, I'll never tire,
I could lose my sight by gazing . . . Oh listen for there are
So many conversations, each wave with a prophetic star!
The story of our love is told by babbling springs
Sharing joy and rapture which the black forest brings,
And evening stars that flicker coldly on firs' black fronds,
The whole earth, the lake, the sky . . . all, all are friends . . .
You could put aside the tiller, you could even drop the oars
And let the current take us wherever it desires,
For wherever we are taken on this watery path
It could only lead to happiness . . . whether in life or death."

Oh, fantasy, often when you and I have been alone
You've lead me into scenery that I have never known!
But have you ever really been to such an enchanted country?
When could it ever have been like that? In the fourteenth century?

Today there's no possibility to lose yourself in her mind,
To caress her when you want to, or be with that girl you find,
Slip your arm round her neck, mouth to mouth, body to body,
Or ask with your eyes only: "Do you love me? Tell me truly!"

Oh, no! Go to touch her and they're knocking at the door,
A whole congress of relations, perhaps an aunt, an uncle — more . . .
You quickly turn your head and glance humbly away . . .
Is there no corner for love in this world today?
And they sit erect on chairs like mummies from Egyptian tombs,
While you roll a cigarette, or sit twiddling your thumbs,
You pluck at your moustache, counting the hairs as you watch her,
Or try to be very knowledgeable on some culinary matter.

I've grown sick of this life . . . not by draining its glasses empty,
But the misery of it all is such bitter prose to me.
Why consecrate with thousands of tears an instinct that's so vain
When it happens to birds and other creatures just the same.
Another controls and inspires us — he's the one that's living,
Laughing through our mouths, is delighted, is whispering,
For lives are like waters that ebb, flow and merge,
Only the river is eternal: The river is the Demiurge.

Haven't you ever felt it wasn't your love? Oh, you fools!
Haven't you ever mistaken the worst things for miracles?
Can't you see that your love is an instrument of nature?
That it's the mere cradle of lives which are only seeds of rancour?
Can't you see that your laughter turns to tears in your sons,
That you inherit the guilt, if Cain still holds influence?
Oh, stage full of puppets . . . mimicry of human speech,
Telling many jokes or tales in a parrot-like screech
With never a thought to what they mean . . . After them an actor
Makes speeches to himself, seeming to repeat forever
What he has told for centuries, and he'll go on like this
Till finally the sun dies in the depths of that abyss.
What? When the moon steals behind clouds, over cosmic deserts,
Why should you follow her, when your world's full of thoughts,
And so slip on silvery-thaw in the snow-iced lanes,
And stare at lighted lamps through glossy window-panes
To see her always beseiged by a bunch of vain idlers,
Head full of frivolous things, smiling at all the loafers?
To hear the rattle of spurs and rustling gowns pass by,
While they twirl their moustaches at the beckoning of an eye?
And when these love agreements conclude at a single glance,
Why should you freeze to death at her gate with that ridiculous stance,
To love her passionately like a child with a stubborn will
When she's as chill and full of whims as the month of April?

Clasping her eagerly in your arms, wasting all your wit,
While longing to admire and caress her from head to foot
As if she were a statue of Paros or a painting by Corregio,
When she's remote and coquettish? You're quite mad, you know . . .
Oh, yes, once I dreamed of a woman who really loved me,
When I sank into deep thought, she'd peer from my shoulder at me,
I'd feel her near, she'd know I loved and understood her . . .
We'd create a romantic novel from our poor life together . . .
But I've given up the search. Why should I try again?
The thirst for eternal stillness always resounds in my brain;
The organ's out of tune — jarring, but the old song's there
Calling at times like a brook spurting in the night air.
And now and again they'll pierce, those purer rays, seen
From a *Carmen Saeculare*, which had also been my dream.
At other times it whistles, shouts, shrieking and scratching
As it plays wildly on the strings, tumultously jostling,
My deserted head burns as the gale blows uncontrolled,
That eternally unfinished song resounding harsh and cold . . .
Are they lost and dumb, those clear life-lines I had?
Ah, the organ's out of tune and the maestro's mad!

The Fifth Satire

The Bible tells how Samson's wife once, at great length,
Planned to cut his hair while he slept, to deprive him of his strength.
And his enemies caught him, bound him tight and put out his eyes,
Proving just what kind of soul the bosom of a dress hides . . .
You lad, who full of dreams are besotted by a woman,
While the golden shield of the moon shines across the common
And stains with strange mysterious stripes the green shadow's throng.
Don't forget, it's your lady's mind that's short, her garments long,
You're elated with fairy visions of a summer night, and say
It exists only for you . . . But — does she feel the same way?
She'll tell you of the ribbons and the fashions *à la mode*,
While your heart is beating out the sacred rhythm of an ode . . .
When the girl coquettishly leans upon your shoulder,
If you have a heart and any sense, remember Delilah.

Certainly, she's beautiful . . . and charming with a child's
Sweet dimples in her cheeks when she laughs or smiles,
And there are dimples in the corner of her murderous lips
And also on her fingers, her legs and her hips.
She isn't small, she isn't large, she isn't thin, but rounding,
So you have something to embrace — just right for loving.
Whatever she says is fashionable, whatever she does becomes her,
And that's how it should be, for beauty will always guide her.
If her conversation's pleasant, her silence is more lovely,

When she says "Leave me alone," her laughter says "Don't really!"
She swings when she walks as if trying to remember a song,
And if she stretches langorously, you'll see it won't be long
Before she rises up on tiptoe so as to reach your mouth,
Imparting with her kiss that strange mysterious warmth
That only the tender soul of a woman can disclose . . .
Oh, that happiness you found in the arms of the one you chose!
You brighten when her cheeks flush, but not with rage —
She's a capricious queen, you seem a childish page —
And looking her straight in the eyes, you'd think you'd now be wise
And learn the real price of life, and what death's price implies.
And seized with the most delightful grief and drunk with joy,
You see her as queen of your mind's world, stupid boy!
So paying deep reverence to those tear-splashed eyelashes,
You imagine her even fairer than some of the goddesses,
And in the chaos of forgetfulness, however much time hurries,
You fall more and more in love with her every day that passes.

What an illusion! Can't you understand, by looking at her face,
That now the smile on her lips is just a habit — a grimace,
That in this world her entire beauty is futile,
And that for no real purpose she makes you lose your soul?
Vainly you play that vaulted lyre's seven stringed harmonies,
As it gathers in its death-howl those long, soft cadences;

Vainly your eyes will mirror old tales' majestic shadows,
Like the ice-flowers that bloom on panes of winter windows
And with heart full of summer, implore. "Devote to me your cares
And the crown of all your thoughts to consecrate with tears!"
How could she understand its not *you* that wants her . . . that there's
A demon within you thirsting for those sweet lights of hers,
A demon that weeps and laughs, yet is unable to hear his grief,
That he only yearns for her . . . to eventually know himself,
That he struggles like a sculptor without arms, and in distress
Is like a maestro grown deaf at that moment of success
When the music's just about to join the astral symphony,
But falls upon his soul in hushed rotating harmony.
And that he doesn't really expect her to die upon the altar
As of old when young girls were sacrificed with a prayer,
Virgins who, having posed as their master's model,
Were then turned into goddesses carved out of marble.

That demon will come to know himself . . . be redeemed,
Discovering himself in his own fire while being consumed,
And in his own tongue, imbued with passions and insatiable love,
He'll break into verse adonic as Horatio does,
He'll capture in his lofty dream the murmuring of the streams,
Damp shadows from the forests, stars that burn as in dreams,
Maybe the beauty of the ancients, in that moment of mystery

Will reappear in his eye, just when he thinks he's happy,
And he'll gaze at her passionately in an act of adoration,
Searching her young eyes, imploring his salvation;
Until the end of time, he'll want her in his arms,
To melt with passionate kisses the ice of her eyes.
If she were made of stone she'd melt with such a fire,
When falling on his knees, he speaks ardently of desire.
Overwhelmed with happiness, he feels he'll lose his reason,
And he loves her all the more in his storm's passion.
But does she know there's a whole world she can give you,
And that by plunging into waves and trying to understand you
She could take the luminous star to fill your heart's abyss?

With the smile of a courtesan and the eyes of an abbess,
She will feign understanding. Yet she'll enjoy the flattery
Of feeling she's the shadow of the earth's eternal beauty.
Say she's a woman among flowers and a flower among women —
That will please her. But make her choose one of the men
From the courting three, swearing love — innocent as she seems —
And you'll see if you watch carefully, how practical she becomes.
And when she grows coquettish and her manner more sprightly,
Sharing words between an old Don Juan, and a dandy,
It's no wonder that her feelings are sometimes misplaced,
Mistaking the knave of spades for the knave of bad taste . . .

For she'll talk like a nun to your devilish desire,
But when the knave of spades appears, her heart's afire,
Her icy gaze is filled with dark thoughts of a lover
And once again she's lively, and places one leg over the other,
For she judges this numbskull as both witty and handsome . . .

To dream that the truth or any other worthless item
Can change a single thing in nature, even a hair follicle,
Is an eternal hinderance and truth's biggest obstacle.

And so, when full of dreams, and besotted by a woman,
While the golden shield of the moon shines across the common
To stain with strange mysterious stripes the green shadow's throng.
Don't forget, it's your lady's mind that's short, her garments long,
You're elated with a fairy vision of a summer night, and say
It exists only for you.
                              But — does she feel the same way?

She'll tell you of the ribbons, and the fashions *á la mode*
While your heart is beating out the sacred rhythms of an ode . . .
So when you see the stone that's neither sorrowful or tender —
If you have a heart and any sense, run fast — it is Delilah!

And when the murmurs . . .

And when the murmurs of my inner thoughts cease,
I sink into the stilled hush of sweet piety —
It's then I want you. So come to me,
Part the cold mist so I can see your face.

And can you lift the power of this night, but gently
With those large eyes, those messengers of peace?
Rise up through the shadows of space
And time so I'll see you coming —
                              Like a dream you come to me!

Come to me slowly . . . nearer and nearer,
Look down into my eyes as you lean over smiling
And if you sigh, I'll know your love is true.

Let your eyelashes near my eyelids linger
So I can sense your heart beating —
Though lost to me, I still worship you.

Gloss

Time goes by, time draws near,
It's all new, it's all old.
What is hidden, what is clear,
Please enquire, then behold;
Have no hope and have no fear,
Every wave will rise and fall;
Just stay cold, remain sincere
If they lure you, if they call.

Much has passed before your gaze,
Many sounds ring in your ear,
Yet who keeps them in thought's maze
Or even bothers to try to hear . . . ?
You, my sweet, should pause anew,
Discover yourself again, my dear,
For despite all the hullabaloo
Time goes by, time draws near.

Don't let the cold balance of thought
Incline its beam to find
That everchanging mask of joy, caught
For only a second,
Given birth at its death knell
Into fleeting pleasure's mould;
For the one who knows it well
It's all new, it's all old.

Now imagine the world a stage,
And you out there the audience;
Despite parts the actor's played
You'll guess his real face.
If he cries or if he argues,
Listen, but don't bend an ear,
Teach yourself from watching his cues
What is hidden, what is clear.

Both the past and the future
Are two sides of the same page,
He who learns them will discover
A beginning's found at the end of an age;
At present we have plenty
Of the new or the old,
But as to their vanity
Please enquire, then behold.

All things that exist today
Suffer the same destiny,
Different masks, but same play,
Other lips, same harmony
And for thousands of centuries
We've laughed or shed a tear;
So you, deluded down the ages,
Have no hope and have no fear.

GLOSS

Have no hope if you see bad men
Building bridges to success,
Even if you were Solomon,
Such rogues will ever surpass,
Have no fear. To get their due
Knave against knave, will always brawl.
So never let them befriend you,
Every wave will rise and fall.

If they touch you move away,
If they curse, then hold your tongue;
Don't give advice whatever they say,
What's the use with a motley throng!
Let them say whatever they want to,
Let them pass, whatever you hear,
But don't let anything persuade you,
Just stay cold, remain sincere.

The world stretches shining nets
Just like a siren's song on the seas;
To replace actors on stage it starts
To tempt you into vortexes;
So stay away from such temptation,
Don't take any notice at all,
Keep only to your own direction
If they lure you, if they call.

If they lure, if you call
Just stay cold, remain sincere,
Every wave will rise and fall,
Have no hope and have no fear,
Please enquire then behold
What is hidden, what is clear,
It's all new, it's all old;
Time goes by, time draws near.

Ode

(In ancient metre)

I never once thought I'd ever learn to die;
Forever young, with my mantle flung about me,
I gazed up dreamily towards that star
    Called loneliness

When suddenly you loomed before me,
You, my torment, painful sweetness . . .
And I drank deep the voluptuousness of death —
    Merciless death.

Now I burn pitiably, tortured like Nessus,
Or like Hercules whose robes were poisoned;
Waters of the oceans could never put out
    Such a fire.

I wail devoured by my own vision,
Swallowed by flames from my own pyre . . .
Shall I rise again luminous from these ashes
    Like the Phoenix?

Let all troubled eyes sink from my sight,
Oh sad indifference come back to my heart;
So I can die serenely, restore me to myself
    Restore me!

Tired Birds

All those sleepy birds
Now tired from flight
Hide among the leaves —
        Good-night!

Only the spring whispers
When the wood sleeps silently;
Even flowers in the gardens —
        Sleep peacefully!

Swans glide to their nest
Sheltering among the reeds —
May angels guard your rest,
        Sweet dreams!

Above a night of sorcery
Comes the moon's graceful light,
All is peace and harmony —
        Good-night!

The Evening Star

Once upon a time if truth be told,
Once in a royal kingdom,
From a noble line in days of old
There lived a beautiful maiden.

No other child had her parents,
And a wonder for her years,
She was the Virgin among the Saints,
The moon among stars.

From the stately arch's shadow
She guides her steps to a corner
Where, through the open window
The Evening Star awaits her.

There she watches out to sea
How he rises and shines,
Pulling his dark ships silvery
Trails on watery plains.

That night she stares, and each night after,
With longing at the sky above,
And he in turn each night sees her
And slowly falls in love.

THE EVENING STAR

As she cradles her arm to pillow her brow
She is lost in dreaming,
Both her heart and her soul now
Cry out with deepest longing.

And every night when he saw her
This gentle star would kindle
When she appeared he was set afire
Upon the shadow of the black castle.

And step by step he follows her
Into the room then glides
To weave there with his cold fire
A spider's web of blaze.

And when the girl is ready to sleep,
He touches the hand on her breast,
Then softly closes her eyelids to keep
Those sweet eyes at rest.

And from the mirror the light poured
Down on her body like a stream
On large eyes pulsing and closed,
On her face turned towards him.

She smiled and seemed to gaze at him
As he trembled through the mirror
For he plunged deeper into her dream
To claim her soul forever.

While talking to this dream of light,
She whispered, sighing deeply,
"Come down, sweet lord, star of my night
Why don't you come? Be near me!

Descend now from the sky, sweet Lord,
Gliding to earth from night,
Come to my room, and to my mind,
To flood my life with light.

While he listened, still flickering
His light was growing stronger,
Then like a flash of lightning
Sank deep into the water.

And the dark sea where he had fallen
Revolved and gently surged
Until a young, handsome man
Majestically emerged.

And with a tall staff in his hand
Adorned with weeds from the sea,
He came to the window and climbed
Over the ledges lightly.

With his long, soft, golden hair,
He seemed a young emperor,
With a bluish shroud held there
By a clasp on his bare shoulder.

And pale as wax was the fine skin
In his translucent grace,
With bright eyes that sparkled in
A handsome dead man's face.

"It was hard to leave my silent sphere
In answer to your prayer,
For the sky is my father here,
And the sea, my mother.

I descended so I could enter your room
And gaze closely upon you,
From the water I was reborn
And left tranquility for you.

Oh, come back with me, my treasure,
Put your world aside!
I am that eternal star,
And you shall be my bride.

I'll take you to coral palaces
An eternity you'll stay
While all the ocean's creatures
Will promise to obey."

"You're as handsome as the angel
Of my dreams, it's true,
But on that path sweet nobleman
I cannot follow you;

Your garments and speech have a strangeness
And your eyes fill me with dread,
For they gleam while still lifeless
I am alive, you are dead."

A day passed, and then three,
Again comes the Evening Star
At night in all his serenity
To gaze down upon her.

And as always when she's dreaming
He is there with her in sleep
And her heart aches with yearning
For her prince of the deep:

"Descend now from the sky, sweet Lord,
Gliding to earth from night,
Come to my room, and to my mind
To flood my life with light!"

And when he heard her tender cry
Pain made his light fade,
And where he perished, again the sky
Began to whirl and rage.

107

The air filled with a red glow
That stretched across the universe,
And moulded from vales of chaos there grew
The shape of a proud face

And his bright crown seemed to burn
On the youth's black hair,
Truth held him as he floated down
Bathed in a halo of fire.

With outstretched arms, like marble
Against the shroud's blackness.
He now walks sad and thoughtful
His face pale in the darkness.

Only his eyes like large fires
Shine intense, magical,
Like two unquenchable desires
So dark and so eternal

"It was so hard to leave my sphere,
To obey took all my might,
The sun is now my father here,
My mother, is the night.

Oh, come back with me, my treasure,
And put your world aside!
I am that eternal Star
And you shall be my bride.

Oh come, let me hang wreaths of stars
Upon your golden hair,
That you may come to light my skies
Brighter and still more fair."

"You're as handsome as the demon
Of my dreams, it's true,
But on that path, sweet nobleman,
I cannot follow you!

Every chord of my breast aches
For your cruel love hurts me,
Like your large and piercing eyes
Whose gaze burns me."

"How could I ever come down so far
And leave my eternity in the sky,
For I am an immortal star
And you alas must die."

"I cannot find the right words
Nor know how to begin,
For though I heard what you said,
I know not what you mean.

But if you want my desire to grow
So I'm betrothed to you,
Then please come down to earth now,
Become a mortal too."

"You ask for my immortality
Just for a lover's kiss,
To prove what you mean to me
And how great my love for you is?

Then yes, I will be born of sin,
And obey a new commandment,
And break free from the bonds of my kin,
And that eternity in the firmament.

And so he went away . . . went away.
Disappeared from above,
Tearing himself from night and day
All for the sake of love.

In the meantime, Catalin,
A sly boy of the household
Who filled the goblets up with wine
While all the guests caroused,

This page who held the regal train
As it draped fold upon fold,
A foundling lad no longer plain
But cunning-eyed and bold,

Round-cheeked, small with a rosy glow
Like peonies in flower,
Watched always hoping to follow
The pretty Catalina.

Oh, she grew more beautiful than ever
With pride in her walk,
Well Catalin, it's now or never
For you to chance your luck.

111

He clasped her waist and touched her hair,
In a corner where it was dark
"What is it you want, Catalin dear?
You should be at your work."

"What do I want? To give happiness,
And love and laughter to you.
So deep in thought! Give me a kiss,
Just one, or perhaps two."

I know nothing of what you speak,
Leave me alone, go away —
It's the Evening Star in the sky I seek,
And dream of night and day."

"If you don't know, I'll teach you
All there is about love,
But please dear, when I caress you,
No temper — quiet, my dove.

As the hunter traps the birds of the air
By setting a net in a tree,
I'll stretch out my left arm here
Then you slip yours round me;

And then like this our eyes must meet,
And stay there, but no blinking . . .
And when I try to lift you off your feet
Rise on your toes, smiling;

And when my face bends down to yours,
Don't turn your head away,
Such loving looks must stay because
Sweet love will grow each day;

And when dear, I start kissing you,
To help you know love better,
If you can then kiss me too,
Our love will be much sweeter."

And as she listened to the boy
Pleased, but surprised,
She shyly and yet gracefully,
Half unwillingly, complied.

She whispered, "We have known each other
Since we were small,
And talkative as one another
We'd suit each other well . . .

113

But you see my star has risen
From the silence of oblivion,
Tracing a vast boundless horizon
To the loneliness of the ocean.

And secretly I hide from him
The tears that spring to my eyes,
When the ebb tide runs to meet him
Or the rough waves rise.

He shines with so much desire
To drive away my sorrow,
And yet he rises higher and higher
Where I can never follow;

In his alien world and a prisoner,
He darts his sad cold ray,
I'll love him forever and forever,
He'll always be far away . . .

And that's why my days are like a wasteland
And long empty hours pass by,
And nights have such a sacred charm and
Yet I know not why."

"But you're still a child, that's why! . . .
Let's hide away in some land,
And time burying our tracks will try
To cover our name with sand;

You'll soon forget even your family,
We'll live so happily together,
And when wise, cheerful, and healthy
You'll dream of your star no longer.

The Star set out. His wings suddenly swelled
To shadow the earth in a moment,
Light years ran back as he passed
And were gone in an instant.

A sky of stars stretched above him,
And a sky of stars below —
As lightning he roamed between them
In a never ending flow.

THE EVENING STAR

Far from cold valleys of forgetting
Surrounded by stillness,
He saw, as in the beginning
Light separated from the darkness.

And then how they surrounded him
On a flood tide as if swimming . . .
He flew, fired by his own passion,
Till again nothing, nothing.

For where he arrives there's no boundary,
Nor eyes able to witness,
And to be born, time strives fruitlessly
From the labour of emptiness.

Here there is nothing and yet there's a thirst
That utterly consumes him,
There is only a great depth traversed
Once more by blind oblivion.

"Father, absolve me, set me free
From the burden of immortal birth,
Then praised forever You will be
By everything on earth;

Oh, ask me Lord, any price
For I need fate's other path,
And all else Lord will I sacrifice,
Giver of life and death;

Take back the immortality
Of my radiance I had above,
And in return please give to me
That first hour of love

From out of chaos, Lord, I came,
And to chaos would return,
And from the stillness I was born
And thirst for stillness again."

"Hyperion, who came from the abyss
To rise with all the universe,
Ask me not for signs and wonders
Without shape, without names.

So you wish to take the shape of man,
And feel the same as them,
But if they perish new waves can
Yet be born again.

117

For only man will chase an ideal,
In vain, but he always tries.
Waves dip to find their graves and still
Other waves will rise.

Only men have lucky stars
But bad luck comes as well
While we have neither time nor place
And hear no death-knell.

In the womb of eternal yesterday
Those who live must die there,
And if a sun fades out today
Another will glow with fire.

They always appear to rise and set,
But death always haunts them,
For things are born to die and yet
Die to be reborn.

While you, when you set will never grow old
But remain Hyperion forever,
For you are from the eternal mould
A miracle and a wonder.

And for whom do you really want to die?
Turn back, return once more
And follow earth with a watchful eye
To see what lies in store."

And so to the celestial night
Hyperion returns
And now, as yesterday, showers his light
As radiantly he burns.

It was in the hazy twilight hour
And night was just beginning;
And from the deep trembling water
The moon was quietly rising

Over the dark paths of the forests
Where her diamonds had been sewn . . .
Under the row of stately limes
Two lovers sat alone.

"O, let my head lean on your breast,
Sweetheart let it lie,
So against your heart I can rest
In the moon's serene eye;

Let the enchantment of her cold light
Enter my life and thought
So that the eternal peace of this night
Will calm the fire you brought.

And so do stay up there above
To soothe all my pain,
For you are my first and only love
And also my last dream."

Hyperion watched and then he knew
The passion their love possessed;
He'd hardly touched her when she drew
His head down to her breast . . .

The silvery petals send sweet rain
To scent the night air
Over the heads of two children
With long, fair hair.

And she, lost in love's ecstasy,
Glances up and sees
Her Evening Star. And whispering shyly
Tells him all her desires.

"Descend now from the sky, sweet Lord,
Gliding to earth from night,
Come to the forest, and to my mind
To bless me with your light!"

He flickers over forest and hill,
Deep in the heart of space,
Guiding the lonely rise and fall
Of waves on the sea's face;

But now from the vast vault of the sky
No longer did he sink to the sea;
"Does it matter mortal shaped from clay,
Whether it's him or me?

You live enchained, and night and day
Destiny waits to unfold,
While I in my own world will stay
Immutable and cold."

Bury that World of Yours in Oblivion

Bury that world of yours in oblivion
And give your whole self to me,
For if our lives are interwoven
No one in the world will see.

Come with me, lost together
Where paths meander, snake-like,
And the forest's restless murmur
Keeps the charmed night awake.

Through the branches stars flicker,
Spreading magical paths before us
And apart from that twinkling silver
No one can even sense us.

Your fine hair's flowing loosely,
So beautiful as it falls about us.
If I hold you, don't deny me,
For no one's going to watch us.

We stand entranced, listening
To the long, low, lament of the horn,
While the moon rises glistening
On the beech woods till dawn.

122

It's answered by the green forest
Under a sad, powerful spell,
And my soul is utterly lost now
Because you are so beautiful.

Half unwilling, half complying,
You want to, and yet you don't,
Compassionate eyes always revealing
That angel's face and heart.

Here is the lake. The full moon
Burnishing its liquid smoothness;
He, kindled by her light, soon
Feels again that loneliness.

Trembling, his rippling foam
Enters the reeds to be comforted,
And even with the world his dream
He finds all sleep has fled.

He brims over with your image.
Then reflects it back to me.
Why do you smile in the water's edge?
You're beautiful, can't you see!

Those evenings of deepest blue
Bend to caress mountain peaks
Showing to me and to you
Glimmering skies, glimmering lakes.

The smell of limes comes from the groves,
Soft is the shadowy willow's lament,
How alone we are in each other's arms
And yet, so content!

In a haze the moon shines through
Pouring her radiance from above
To find me embracing you,
My sweet, my fair-haired love.

And If

And if the boughs beat the pane
And poplar trees shiver,
You're there in my mind again
Slowly coming nearer.

And if the stars beat down
On the lake to light its depths,
It's to soothe every pain
And calm all my thoughts.

And if the thick clouds part
To let the full-moon through,
It's so I'll keep you in my heart
And be eternally with you.

126

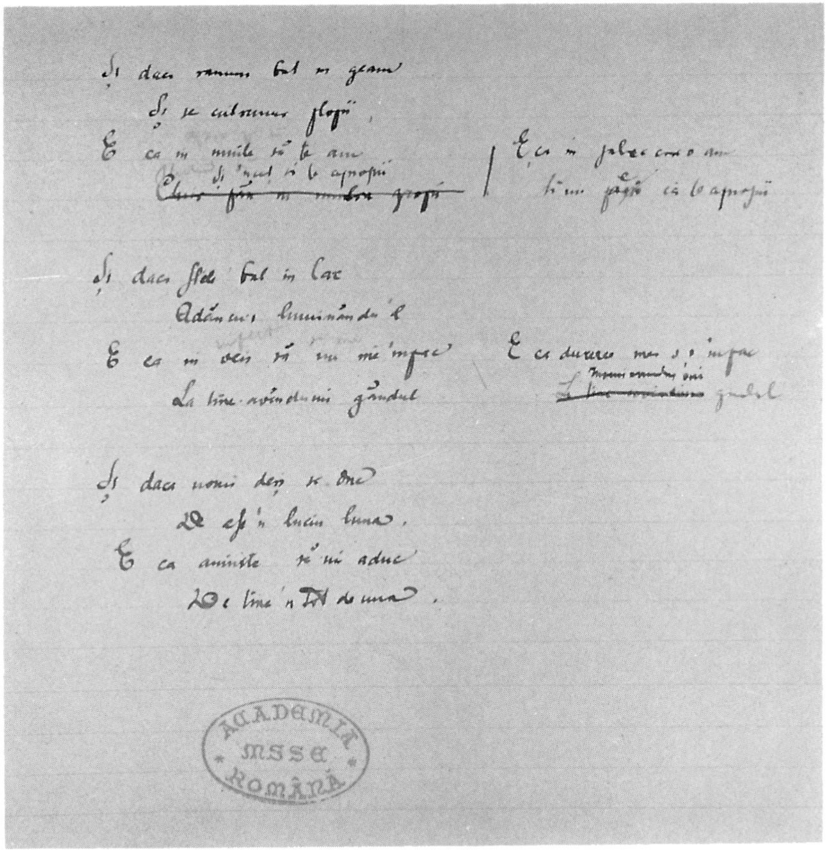
Şi dacă ramuri bat în geam
Şi se cutremur plopii,
E ca în minte să te am
Şi 'ncet să te apropii

E ca în ... să te am
... să te apropii

Şi dacă stele bat în lac
Adâncu-i luminându-l
E ca în ochi să-mi mi-împac
La tine avându-mi gândul

E ca durerea mea s-o împac
... gândul

Şi dacă norii deşi se duc
De es'n luciu luna,
E ca aminte să mi aduc
De tine 'ntotdeauna.

The manuscript of Şi dacă.

From that Star

The radiance from that new-born star
Will take many thousands of years
To travel a path that comes so far
To finally reach our eyes.

Perhaps it died while on its way
Through infinite blue space,
Yet only now does its light stray
To shine upon your face.

Slowly climbing the dark skies
Is the dead star's icon:
Invisible when it did exist,
Today, we see an illusion.

And so it is when passion's fled
Lost in the depths of night,
The light of our love, now dead,
Still haunts us in its flight.